Timberline of the Mind

Poems by

Garry Wade McGiboney, Ph.D.

Reveltree Publishing and Distribution

Timberline of the Mind

Copyright © 2018 by Garry Wade McGiboney, Ph.D.

Cover design by Star Winter Design. All rights reserved.

Published by Reveltree Publishing, an imprint of Marlborough MasterClass Printing LLC, New York, Dublin, and London

783949218ka298

Without limiting the rights of the above copyright, no part of this publication may be reproduced, stored in or introduced into a retrieval system, or transmitted in any form, or by any print or electronic means without the express permission of the copyright owner or publishers.

Library of Congress Cataloging-in-Publication Data
British Library Cataloguing-Publication Data
Irish Library Cataloguing Association
Print ISBN – 978-0-9979629-4-9
Library ISBN – 0690455019

First Edition by Garry Wade McGiboney © 2018
Timberline of the Mind
1. Poetry
2. Literature

Printed and distributed in the United States by Reveltree Publishing Distribution and in the UK by MasterClass Printing. LLC

TABLE OF CONTENTS

Preface 1
A Baseball in the Woods 44
A Child's Love 120
A Fine Summer's Day 123
A Spirit Forever Strong 58
About His Life 80
Abstraction 71
Alone 26
Another Type of Dark 38
Anymore 54
Anticipation 114
Bears Her Mind 56
Bi-Polar 27
Book Soul 8
Cabinet of Curiosities 32
Care 34
Caretaker 33
Change Cannot Feel the Warm 135
Churchill 69
Circles in My Mind 137
Clouds See 5
Dignity and Grace 127
Distortion 128
Does it Matter; Does it Vary? 41
Dolphin and the Sea 112
Don't Give Up 29
Doubt 102
Echoes of Halls 92
Embarrassed 66
Empty 138
Empty Hands 20
Everyday Knights 65
Everywhere 53
Feral 30
Field of Sorrow 125

Finding What Was Never Lost 12
From Far Away 124
Go 46
Growing Old 45
Hallucinations Alone 108
Heart to Try 73
Her Mother Cries 19
Her Smile 109
Hero or Fraud 36
His Way 130
Idea 107
Insanity 43
Ireland 61
Irish Island by the Irish Sea 88
Island of Green 118
It Can Be Done 91
It Flies Again 37
It Now Was 24
J.D. 85
John Ronald and Clive Staples 84
Last Day 22
Last to See 10
Low 89
Maggie 78
Make Warm Sounds 48
Marched Into Legend 64
Mary Cassatt 96
Mind Melts 104
Music Breathes 35
My Friend 68
My Imagination Settled Into Sleep 60
Never There 28
No Name 9
Not Yet 79
Nurse 121
Once Upon a Time 90
Orange Cat 75
Original Matter 49

Pain	67
Perfect Shape	87
Place of Peace	101
Politics and Children	119
Priceless Time	111
Proud	95
Purpose	113
Purred and Pawed	97
Quiet but Not Silent	93
Reality Room	131
Saint-Gaudens' Adams Memorial	63
Sanctuary	13
Senator	106
Share His Smile	100
She Waits by the Door	99
She Said	135
Sleep and Busy	55
Song of Whitman	15
Sounds of Noise	62
Storyteller	83
Sun and Wind	51
Sunday Fear	115
Sunrise, Sunset	72
Sure You Will	82
That Season, The Soldiers	16
The Ache	129
The Air is Missing	17
The Baseball Card	31
The Island	57
The Last Time	117
The Line	7
The Little Boy is Bad	70
The Oak Tree of Life	81
The Painting	4
The Purpose	11
The Room	39
The Sandpiper	105
The Statue	21

The Top	42
They Wait	18
Thinking	135
Tight	6
Timberline of the Past	14
Time	50
Time Matters	122
Time to Go	110
Time versus Space	86
Tough	40
Tree and Silence	103
Tree Top	23
Unborn	25
Unfamiliar Woods	3
Virus among Us	74
Waif of Foreboding	94
War Life	132
Warmth	59
We're Old Cats	116
Where Did the Sun Go?	47
Where Do the Shadows Go?	52
Where He Lived	77
Why Do We Forget?	76
Why Does It Have To End?	98

Preface

Many years ago, I suffered a traumatic brain injury (TBI) from an auto accident, not of my making. I was unconscious and experienced three grand mal seizures during the ambulance ride to the traumatic care emergency center. During the months following the accident, I had periodic amnesia. Also, I had rehabilitation sessions with a speech and language therapist, a physical therapist, and an occupational therapist for several months. While recovering, I had daydreams and nightmares where images and words tumbled together in a kaleidoscope that I could not understand. My occupational therapist was the most sympathetic and insightful. Some said the unusual images and prismatic nature of my illusions represented my brain's efforts to sort out the sensory damages, but the occupational therapist heard and saw something different. She suggested that I write about the thoughts and images in order to better understand them; so quietly and secretly I did. Some of the thoughts were simple, common everyday observations of life but from very different perspectives and yet others were from an unknown place in my mind.

As my memory recovered and my brain healed, thoughts of books, poems, and people came forth in unusual and unfiltered ways, while images, colors, shapes, and memories folded across my mind in unusual if not bizarre patterns. I described many of them through writing, but I never looked back over them nor attempted to do anything with them. Writing about them seemed to serve a need of the moment and no other purpose.

Recently, while pushing through some difficult times and sorting through my files, I found my notes from the post-TBI days. The material was interestingly unfamiliar and yet familiar, too. I wondered if I could capture those same observations of life in a more contemporary mind and blend the old and the new together. The result is this book of poetry. The poems represent the mind of a person struggling to recover physically, spiritually, and emotionally combined with present-day feelings and observations of our internal and external lives from a mind that was damaged and then healed.

The title of the book was not chosen at random. The poem *Timberline of the Past* resonated with my purpose. A timberline is a line or altitude above which no trees grow. The timberline is usually a point where there is a lack of enough oxygen, warmth, or water to keep trees alive. Each of us has a timberline of the mind above which our lives, physical and emotional conditions, our experiences, attitude, and ability to cope are not sufficiently nurtured enough to reach a place where we are content and truly happy.

Let's visit those places above the timberline of the mind.

Unfamiliar Woods

The view from the woods to the house is unfamiliar.

All that I know is not visible and unfamiliar.

The sun's streaks through the woods cast shadows unfamiliar.

While the silence of the woods consumes the sounds that are unfamiliar.

There is a strange lure of the woods that keeps me there, the caress of the unfamiliar.

A view of the familiar from the unfamiliar.

The Painting

The painting stares back at me.

She doesn't even know my name but she stares at me.

Am I the observer or is she observing only me?

I think I hear the sounds in the painting asking about me.

I turn away but I feel her breath and eyes on me.

She stays in my mind and I know she's waiting for me.

Clouds See

What do clouds see?

Do they look down or look up to see?

Do clouds listen to what lies between what they see?

Clouds change shape not from the wind but from what they see.

A world formless and shapeless to those who do not see.

In the world of clouds shaping and shifting it's the whisper of what to see.

Tight

She holds the little book tight.

It's her world tonight; she must hold it tight.

The dark shadows do not care; they only grip her tight.

Her dreams hold her heart and make things right when they hold her tight.

This night without end with shadows fading in and out grips her soul tight.

How can she drift away without a trace and free heart and hope tied tight?

Her little book hugs her tight.

The Line

She goes through the line and waits in line.

It's what she does every day in step and in line.

She cannot drift out of line.

It forms as the beginning and the end of the line.

But the messages are blurred more often than not in the narrow line.

She gives in and becomes the line.

Book Soul

The book has a soul and reaches out.

It's been too many places, been touched and left out.

Like a child desperate for a warm touch, the book reaches out.

It cannot feel any worth or purpose when inert and left out.

Take the book; hold it; consume it; talk with it; explore it inside and out.

A book has no soul when it's left out.

No Name

Birds with no names cannot sing.

They fly from tree to bush, following the rays of the sun but cannot sing.

Their feathers pale in color because the no-name bird cannot sing.

Higher she flies looking for a name; the touch of the sky but no name; the bird cannot sing.

A light may shine on its feathers and a soft voice must call its name or the bird cannot sing.

Last to See

The feeling is too strong to ignore; the light too dim to see.

The shadow plays against the wall; the wall sheds its eyes to see.

He hides his feelings, again, beneath the transparent clothing that no one but everyone can see.

See the feelings; see the loss; see the pail empty with purpose and wait for the moment to see.

The tight grip slips away; the last grasp slips off; the last to see.

The Purpose

It is a war within and without – too slow to be fast to end.

The smell of war like the smell of moss invades to the end.

Shaking and trembling with the heart of purpose of the sacrifice at the end.

The end does not matter because the beginning was magic until the end.

Smiling in pain; smiling in loss; smiling for the purpose was the end.

Finding What Was Never Lost

The philosopher said God is dead and mankind drifts.

Shades of sand and currents of tides find a rightful place in drifts.

Finding what was never lost the philosopher cannot see, blinded by the thought of drifts.

Bring him back; point to the source – the philosopher is sinking in the drifts.

Show him the stars that blink out; the grass he cannot feel; his soul in the drifts.

Sanctuary

Come ashore and see the sanctuary of lights.

It brightens even the night, the lights.

The shadows slip away and glance back longing at the lights.

They are warm; the lights are soft and hard; they are your lights.

Don't look away; never look away – the eyes of the lights are your lights.

Timberline of the Past

The timberline holds fast to the past.

It will not let new faces and paces steal the line of the past.

The past holds the roots and runners in place for hope of the past.

A past that the god of the present abhors and deplores because it's the past.

Breach the timberline the present shouts, nothing to gain from the past.

But the present's fatigue grows; one cannot fight both the present and the past.

Song of Whitman

Leaves of Grass, the song of Whitman and a song for all who want to see.

The words form around memories building a cocoon of regrets and promises we see.

But the song rings true of what can still be and what we can still see.

The captain of our soul awakens to the call and pulls back the mist for us to see.

More than words, the song sings for all time for anyone who still aches to see.

That Season, The Soldiers

I walked over the sacred grounds covered with the grass of the season.

It was so long ago the memories don't matter, the losses were just part of the season.

Looking back after I stumbled, I saw nothing there but did I feel the upward push of that season?

Who spoke to me? Who tried to say "I'm here?" Who made me look back? It was that season.

I was reminded that the memory for them is all they have left – the reason for the season.

The Air is Missing

The hall is not long but it seems longer – the image narrows but the hall widens.

It's not closer but it's not moving away and the air is missing as the fear widens.

Each step is deeper and slower but the inevitable comes speedily and widens.

Wrapped in fear but cuddled in soft whispers, hope widens.

Awakened by sun streaks or pain. The air is back. Breath widens.

They Wait

The cemetery birds watch and wait.

The sad procession drifts up the hill like a wisp of thin smoke and then they wait.

They all look down as you look at them. Silently they said to wait.

But your silent scream raises your head away from them and into the sky to wait.

The sky; the changing sky fades to orange and black streaks to wait.

But the wait is over and no one knows, even those that wait.

Her Mother Cries

The baby smiles and her mother cries.

The baby sees her mother and her mother cries.

The baby feels her mother's touch and her mother cries.

The baby hears her mother's voice and her mother cries.

The baby feels her mother's love even when her mother cries.

Empty Hands

The god grasped the throne with both hands.

Yelling down from the cloud kingdom to mortals below, he makes fists with both hands.

The thunder blooms and booms; the lightning angers the sky; the god has blood on his hands.

Idolatry holds no claim on his anger; ignorance is only a paint without color in his hands.

But idleness gathers the storm clouds and rips through the god's heart with empty hands.

The Statue

It stands tall and is admired by all.

It is the center of conversation and embraced by all.

Even strangers claim it as their own with all.

Where did it come from – the cry goes out to all.

Quickly it fads from eyes and minds and becomes oblivious to all.

Now the interest is gone; no one sees it though it stands erect; it's blind to them all.

Last Day

She said I need it to make it through the day.

Though no was there to hear her protest that day.

She insisted it was hers to keep and take all day.

Nothing else in her life would do what she needed that day.

With no one there to look into her eyes; it was her last day.

Tree Top

No one can see it except the birds, but even the birds pay no mind.

It's always there so why mind?

It's always been there and always will so what mind?

In storms and winds and through dark cold nights it doesn't mind.

Thinking of the top of the tree that no one sees or thinks about is on my mind.

It Now Was

C.S. Lewis said it wasn't there and then it was.

The angels circled his mind and saw what it was.

His soul was left at the Battle of the Somme, sadly it was.

Not even a god could cope and survive as bad as it was.

But a light found him and where it wasn't it now was.

Unborn

She smiles into the light.

She can't see but she hears through the light.

She feels the heartbeat and touch through the light.

She reaches toward the light.

It's so close somewhere in the light.

Just out of reach in the light.

Just out of reach in the fading light.

The light. Reaching the light.

The Idea

The idea came without an invitation.

Not fully formed but persistently without an invitation.

It won't go away; it flutters and bites; it hovers in flight without an invitation.

Filling the spaces around it does no good even without an invitation.

Let it go; let it be; let it grow; let it flow without an invitation.

Bi-Polar

Not so fast.

It cannot last when it's that fast.

It swirls and spins much too fast.

It sinks and dips, plummets and soars high and fast.

The fall is steep, deep, and fast.

Much too fast; low and high much too fast.

Never There

The smile and touch faded away as if never there.

But the longing for the smile and touch remains there.

The cold embrace is a routine; the love is not there.

The needs and desires are a wistful dream; the touch will never be there.

It will never be there; maybe it never was there.

Don't Give Up

Fighting, struggling, you cannot give up.

Life is about not giving up.

There is nothing else except not giving up.

It's all there to reason and curse but not to give up.

Give up and see eyes fade; give up and others give up.

Yell at the sky; stomp the dirt; scream at gods and God, just don't give up.

Feral

Feral but free.

Hungry but free.

Lonely but free.

Afraid but free.

Cold but free.

Wet but free.

Freedom isn't free.

The Baseball Card

He is young, athletic, and filled with promises.

The picture on the card is fading promises.

The card with worn edges of promises.

Where did it all go? Where are the promises?

With dry tears, he puts the baseball card back in the drawer with his other promises.

Cabinet of Curiosities

The curiosities are in the cabinet.

The broken wing of an ancient bird fills the cabinet.

An eye curious to the world and looking out while others look in the cabinet.

The touch hot and cold, wet and coarse recoils from the cabinet.

It was there in the corner waiting, blending with the shadows, watching from the cabinet.

Always, eternally watching from the cabinet.

Caretaker

Someone waits for the family to leave: what does he think?

Someone lowers the dirt; what does he think?

Someone puts the marker on the grave; what does he think?

Someone trims the grass in the cemetery; what does he think?

Someone removes the withered flowers; what does he think?

Someone sees the number of visitors diminish: what does he think?

Someone sees the grave abandoned: what does he think?

Someone sees no one: what does he think?

Someone sees that no one sees: what should he think?

Care

How does he sit there pretending to care?

Asking questions that don't matter because he doesn't care.

It's all for show and polls, not due to care.

The mirror stares back and he looks to the side and says to himself, "I do care."

But, no, he doesn't care; he won't care; but at one time he did care.

Where did the care go? Awash in glory; awake in misery because he doesn't care.

Music Breathes

The music dances in her head and in her soul but the paper is blank.

Does she see the music and feel the notes in her hand or does her mind go blank?

It starts with a note; it moves to a score; the momentum and then her blink goes blank.

Too much to capture; too many images to feed; too many rhythms to feel, but it's all blank.

It comes again when she's lost in a dream and she runs to the piano because it's no longer blank.

She softly caresses the music and it breathes; she gives it birth and life to that which was blank.

Hero or Fraud

A philosopher or a fraud?

A saint or a fraud?

A teacher or a fraud?

An atheist or a fraud?

A Christian or a fraud?

One or the other; one cannot be both a hero and a fraud.

It Flies Again

The Phantom lifts angrily into the sky again.

It trails streams of death's steam and looks for victims again.

Its shape is poured from the cast of warlords hurdling toward war again.

It maneuvers like a young eagle on the hunt again.

The rains of destruction come from the bowels of the Phantom time and time again.

It feels no pain; it feels no guilt, and even when wounded it dreams of flying again.

Another Type of Dark

He didn't notice that the sun had set and the room is dark.

The only light he needs is the screen light in the dark.

The device is his link to the world and keeps him from the dark.

But is it light in the dark or just another type of dark?

The Room

What happens to an empty room?

Once filled with energy and laughter and tears, now it's just a room.

The bed is long empty with a light layer of dust in the quiet room.

Sunlight peeks through the curtains looking for the child in the motionless room.

The air is empty in the room.

They all wait - the toys, the books, the dolls, the dreams, but it knows - the room.

Years upon years, tears over tears, emptiness is now the purpose of the room.

Tough

Delicate but tough.

Little girls and butterflies prance and dance but are tough.

They move without effort and land where they want to be gentle or tough.

Scoop up the nectar, smell the air and then dive into the depths to be tough.

Climb the stars and reach with your heart and learn what is soft and what is tough.

Tender and tough. Always be tender and tough

Does it Matter; Does it Vary?

It all adds up and never varies.

On land or sea in a book or in French it never varies.

Stretch it, bend it, throw it down or throw it up it never varies.

Cuss it, squeeze it, hold your head above it – it doesn't matter because it never varies.

Write in ink, pencil, or rock morning, noon, and night it never varies.

The answer is always the same; it never varies.

The Top

Clear to the bottom and from the bottom to the top.

Shallow but deep, narrow but wide – it must be clear at the top.

Clearing back the water with your hands touches the spirit all the way to the top.

It passes by without a nod, by now it is miles away cresting to the top.

Reaching up to peek over the edge rides the current to the drop just before the top.

A Baseball in the Woods

I found an old baseball deep in the woods.

The once perfect shape and purpose were changed by the woods.

Someone held it once and brought it deep into the woods.

Was it left because it held too many memories even in the woods?

The stitches are torn and the leather is mold but it's still a baseball in the woods.

A baseball that a little boy once held in his hands and close to his heart, now in the woods.

Take it home or leave it there, I struggled with the thought while in the woods.

I left what I found because it's someone's past; someone left it there to forget in the woods.

Insanity

Sanity is not so great.

A little lunacy goes a long way and is great.

Worry melts away and images form in awkward shapes that are great.

The touch is tasty and the taste smells of incense that is great.

Dreams of day and night are interwoven and purge the sane mind which is great.

I don't need your sympathy; my madness fits me great.

Wait, madness bubbles and my mind slips on a peel; maybe insanity is not so great.

Growing Old

No one said it was an easy thing to do.

But at one time it seemed like the natural thing to do.

It led from one day to the next and no turn or twist changed the thing to do.

No joy no sorrow changed the thing to do.

As it grew nearer the vision took shape and as did the thing to do.

Without effort she grew old; that was the thing to do.

Go

There is always somewhere to go.

Whether or not we need to go.

Something pulls us to stay on the go.

Quiet solitude scares people on the go.

People run from soft silence; they must go.

They must go; they cannot sit still; they are on the go.

People miss it every day, a moment of silence during the busy day on the go.

Where Did the Sun Go?

Where have you been and what did you do?

Your warmth was gone and no knew where you were or what to do.

We looked everywhere even behind the clouds and we didn't know what else to do.

You wouldn't be in the lake or low in a cave, so we asked the trees what to do.

There you were all warm in the trees, shining and showing us what to do.

Make Warm Sounds

Does she know that her skilled hands made a child happy today?

The gloves caressed and warmed her tiny fingers today.

She turns them; she claps them together to make warm sounds today.

She cries until her mom found the lost one today.

One day they no longer fit but secretly in her pocket, she keeps one close today.

Does she know that her skilled hands comforted a little girl yesterday and a young lady today?

Original Matter

Original matter.

Is the origin matter primordial matter are divine matter?

And the world goes round while tempers flare that do not matter.

They carry banners and pray out loud and others hide behind science and its matter.

A common purpose doesn't matter.

Harassment, fighting, and accusations replaced original matter.

Time

Waiting with time.

My companion and friend is time.

It is with me all the time.

Despondent or euphoric, bored or thrilled, it always has time.

Its shape is unknown and it quietly stands by at any time.

To some people, it is the ever-present oppressor marking against their time.

I'm content waiting here with time.

Sun and Wind

Wind and sunshine work their magic.

The sun shimmering off the leaves goes unnoticed until the wind weaves its magic.

The sun is bright on the still waters but comes to life with the breath of the winds magic.

Snow aglow with streaks of sunlight and whirling wind turns into kaleidoscope magic.

On calm days the sun shines less bright with dim magic.

But the sun comes to life when the wind spins around and pulls the sun into its magic.

Where Do the Shadows Go?

Where do the shadows go?

They see us before we see them but in the dark where do they go?

They run to us and stretch far away when the sun bends around to see them go.

We think we see shadows in the dark and laugh away the thought as we go.

But there was a shadow in the dark waiting to reach up to you as you go.

They are dark and serious; light and gay; long and short, and they come and go.

Where do the shadows go?

Everywhere

I'm not here or there but I'm everywhere.

I move from place to place without moving everywhere.

Look closely and quickly because I appear nowhere and then everywhere.

I'm in front of you and behind you, at the same time while you look everywhere.

I'm both everything and nothing and everywhere.

Anymore

Laughter doesn't smile here anymore

Laughter doesn't sing here anymore.

Laughter doesn't play here anymore.

Laughter doesn't grow here anymore.

The little boy doesn't live here anymore.

Sleep and Busy

Sleep chased me when I was young and busy.

It wrapped its arms around me to keep me warm when I was busy.

Sleep tugged on my mind and I chased it away, too busy.

Now I look for sleep to soften the memories of the days when I was busy.

Sleep slips away behind the shadows and is too busy.

I reach for it; I ache for its relief now while I'm busy.

Sleep hides and my soul cannot rest when my mind is so restlessly busy.

Bears Her Mind

She lifts her soul and bears her mind.

She commits to no one and gives everyone her mind.

She cannot claim it as her own but she holds it close in her mind.

She cannot share it fully and keep her mind.

She touches it lightly and smiles; it doesn't mind.

The Island

An island not far away that no one knows.

A shroud of mystery hangs low over the island that no one knows.

Long, lonely beaches through the ages that no one knows.

It longs for someone to touch the water, feel the sand, and embrace what no one knows.

Each day like the last. Each future like the past. Nothing changes and no one knows.

It fads a little each day. A place no one knows.

A Spirit Forever Strong

She's brilliant, beautiful, and strong.

Her soft green eyes and unruly thick hair project a carefree nature but she's strong.

Time may be swift and the winds blow cold and damp but her will is hot and strong.

Touches and kindness rule her heart and her passion is strong.

It's not enough to feel love and hold tight and strong.

She looks into the unknown, seeking a spirit forever strong.

Warmth

Warmth is in the cold air and strong wind.

It's looking for a place to land but is swirled around by the playful wind.

The cold pushes and teases and pushes it out into the wind.

Cold wants to play and tosses it up into the air caught by the wind.

All living things watch and wait for the dance to end; warmth will come again and come on the wind.

My Imagination Settled Into Sleep

Did the pen move on its own?

It was here not there when last I looked on my own.

I cannot write so I straighten all the pens that I own.

There, it moved again on its own.

I didn't touch or bump the table to make it move; it's on its own.

My imagination settled into sleep; will the pen write on its own?

It moved; it turned and said, "You're on your own."

Can psychosis be far away if the words form together on their own?

Then psychosis it will be; my imagination has abandoned me and left me on my own.

Ireland

The land is ancient, older than light.

The island was carved by blue ice before life gave light.

It gouged; it burrowed; it sliced; it sculptured the land to hold the light.

The blue faded as the green grew with the light.

Through the ages the green has shifted and transformed, creating many greens of light.

The green island of many colors; the green island that cradles the light.

Sounds of Noise

Abandon the noise.

It comes under the door and creeps through the window, the noise.

Sounds of metal, sounds of steel – sounds of noise.

It grows louder and invades my senses; why can't they turn off the noise.

At night, during the day, quiet mornings no longer exist in the noise.

Abandon it, I say; give it wide berth and send it away with people who want the noise.

Now it's quiet. I can hear my thoughts – bring back the noise.

Marched Into Legend

They ran into danger and marched into legend.

No one cared and no one knew they would be legend.

They lost companions for cause and faith and all became legend.

No one remembers but the land and the sky, witnesses to the legend.

Legends alive or is it a myth? Life gives into a faded memory, not a legend.

The soldiers lived and died without thinking about their legend.

Over the landscape of time, they marched into legend.

Saint-Gaudens' Adams Memorial

The face is alive with sadness and despair.

The body is folded beneath a blanket of despair.

The haunting beauty is ancient but young with ageless despair.

She wears it sadly but gracefully with cloth made of despair.

The sculpture's hands moaned softly with each curve carved out of despair.

Now she sits quietly wrapped in time and caressed by despair.

Everyday Knights

Tenderness and severity of the noble knights.

MacDonald's vision in *Phantastes* was filled with fierce and true knights.

But MacDonald said the everyday man possesses the will and the might of sturdy knights.

Look to the cause and strength in their hearts. Any man and woman can be the knights.

To the rescue in small ways or through a mighty cause, it's the will and the heart that make knights.

The knights in *Phantastes* and all other stories cannot match the soul in everyday knights.

Embarrassed

I didn't know whether to curse or cry.

Embarrassment is a terrible thing in front of others;
curse or cry.

It's binary state: curse or cry.

But there should be a third option, but running away
is worse than curse or cry.

Our mind, soul, and heart crash into each other
during such times arguing whether to curse or cry.

Pain

My face paled from the pain.

It stole my heart and crushed my soul with pain.

Medicate they said; cast away that crawling, gnawing pain.

Give in and dope up; it's the noble way to handle pain.

They said that's what everyone does when they have pain.

But when the pain is gone, the numbness replaces the pain.

That's only natural so medicate that too, just like you did for the pain.

My face paled again; creeping back is the pain - a different, deeper pain.

Live or be driven by numbness and pain – the modern day dilemma of pain.

My Friends

My companions, my friends can see me.

My companions, my friends can touch me.

My companions, my friends can hear me.

My companions, my friends understand me.

My companions, my friends - my books sustain me.

Churchill

In the blackest night of nights, he saw a small light.

The light was in his heart and his soul burned like a bright light.

Others saw darkness and gave up all hope of light.

Still, others sold their inner nobility to sacrifice the light.

He shone brightest and noblest and the darkest moments never extinguished his light.

The world would see his light.

The world would be drawn to his light.

The world would survive by his light.

The darkness gave way to his light.

The Little Boy is Bad

The little boy is bad.

His behavior is out of control and disrespectfully bad.

He should be kicked out of school because he's bad.

Don't tell me he might be sad; this boy is just plain bad.

Don't say he can't see or hear or speak, 'cause he's just plain bad.

There is only one way to handle him when he is that way – punish the bad.

Take your time to fix your hair; take time to watch your show, but punish him now 'cause he's bad.

Teach the subjects and pat the others on the back but scold him because he's bad.

He came into the world bad, and there is nothing to do but to beat down the bad.

That quiet moment was absurd because he is relentlessly bad.

He plays the role that he knows so well. He can't be good for being so bad.

Abstraction

The abstract thought and image visit me each day and night.

No rhyme, no rhythm, no substance, no purpose day or night.

It lingers without noise; it asks for nothing and yet it blooms at night.

It burned bright last night and kept sleep away; it tries to find voice especially in the night.

I listen and watch looking for the message in the abstraction during the night.

The shadow on the wall is not from an object in my room; it's from the abstraction.

Abstraction – talk to me or show me the way. A soft voice from far away said, "You're almost there; listen to the night."

Sunrise, Sunset

I believe what I feel and know what I think.

But loss of life, loss of love, and loss of hope make me think.

There may not be an order or destiny or gods or a God that make me think.

Maybe we are adrift to find our own way, depending only on how we think.

The sunrise and sunset hold no promise or fear because it's just another day, I think.

Heart to Try

Go ahead and try.

Use your power and influence to make others cry so they won't even try.

You think your status was nobly bestowed and you wear it like a crown and dare others to try.

Your humble start; your failures tempered your spirit and hardened your heart to try.

Others can get their own; you owe them only scorn, a path to honor is there if they'll only try.

Are you a true self-worshipper and everything is made by you? Someday give awareness a try.

A day will come of loneliness and isolation because you did not try.

It takes a heart to try.

Virus among Us

The just don't like us, the virus among us.

They come back every year to infect us.

They hide as micro-shape shifters and come after us.

They are vengeful and unforgiving and tear at even the healthiest among us.

The science works against them but every year the virus prevails against us.

Sick as we might be, and as evil as the virus appears, the fight is still in us.

But the persistent virus hides around each corner waiting with a blanket to drape over us.

Orange Cat

The old orange cat showed up one hungry day.

The sad look, matted fur, and slow walk said it's another lonely, hungry day.

Afraid to come close but he was hopeful I would keep him from enduring another hungry day.

His orange, aged eyes were sad beyond bearing; the meow weak from another hungry day.

He dashed to the food and I slipped away but he sadly looked up and did not eat on this hungry day.

Confused, thinking he was too ill to eat, I bent down to offer a soft voice on his hungry day.

He ate gently and thoroughly but he stopped each time I moved away on his hungry day.

Then I saw the depth of his sadness; it wasn't just hunger for food; it was a hunger for caring on this hungry day.

I sat on the ground nearby and the old orange cat ate every bite on his hungry day.

Why Do We Forget?

I wonder why we so easily forget.

The pain is always real and lasts as if we'll never forget.

The fresh memories flood back without warning to remind us not to forget.

But we forget.

We forget what we loved; we forget what we cherished; we forget.

It's not the heart that forgets; it's not the soul that forgets; it's our life that forgets.

Without moments of solitude our lives crowd the memories out and we forget.

Quiet tears flow when a memory surrounds us; not tears of the past but because we forget.

Where He Lived

Does it matter that he lived?

He worked hard all of his life; a strong and simple man as he lived.

Carved from the cold stone of poverty where he lived.

Cruelty was common as a child; it was the way everyone lived.

Some grew bitter and mean; some grew better and kind as they lived.

Every day was endless work with few moments of rest and many nights of worry where he lived.

The family was first and he prayed when he could but work was a life where he lived.

He quietly passed away; who noticed or cared; his marker is bare; his field untilled where he lived.

Who even knows that he lived?

Maggie

She was tiny, smart, energetic, happy, and free.

Her joy was shared by everyone; she made them feel happy and free.

One day her eyes darkened and her smile went away; she struggled to stay free.

Her fever soared while everyone's hopes drowned; her tiny spirit ached to be free.

With heads held low and tears flowing, the tiny girl's spirit fought to be free.

She saw a small light and her spirit sprinted to it; her eyes brightened and she was free.

She runs through our lives with smiles and hugs; now we know what it means to be free.

Not Yet

Hold on; wait; it's not time yet.

Cold days and nights are certainly coming back; don't bloom yet.

But the flowers and trees and birds and children want the spring; Mother Nature says, "Not yet."

The breath of fresh air, the warmth in the winds make Old Man Winter blink but he says "Not yet."

Sleeping peacefully dreaming of the next warm day, winter steals the night and makes sure it's not yet.

Arising cold and trembling and feeling the light touch of snow, spring shivered and knew not yet.

About His Life

Drifting slowly to the surface like the last day of life.

The sun is not as bright or warm as before in his life.

Over the years he was settling to the bottom and didn't know that about his life.

He thought it was just part of living, part of life.

Some live to live and some live to die; his life was neither; he didn't feel life.

Floating on the surface face down like settling on the bottom face up is not life.

Now it doesn't matter; it's the last day of his life.

The Oak Tree of Life

Majestic and strong against the storms and wind.

It stands tall for decades deep in the hundred acre woods as a friend of the wind.

Home to creatures with scurrying lives and to those lifted by the wind.

The first to feel the sun's touch and the warmth of a new day in the wind.

Untouched by famine or worries about man's world and wars in the wind.

Each day is life filled and the promise of life carried by the wind.

It has deep roots and lives on sun and rain; listen - its life can be heard on the wind.

Sure You Will

Alone in her will and against her will.

Easier to walk away and work at will.

But the allure, the need is part of her will.

Her soul has blended with her will.

The need is a hunger stronger than will.

So she sits alone, night and day, calling upon her will.

When she walks away, it's not far because she is pulled back by her will.

When she completes her story she's always surprised by the duration of her will.

The will to continue through doubt and loneliness strengthens her will.

I can't start another one, she cries to herself; but her soul and heart say, "Sure you will."

Storyteller

She's a storyteller; her voice is an ebb and flow.

The children gather around and move closer to hear her story flow.

The adults smile detached but her voice catches their heart and pulls them into the flow.

Now everyone in the room is entranced by her voice and how it becomes the flow.

The story and her voice become one in the story's flow.

She finishes with a story within the story to forever keep the flow.

It was more than a story; it was more than a storyteller's tale; it is life's flow.

John Ronald and Clive Staples

His intellect was unsurpassed and he was blessed with a good heart.

He went to war and was broken deep in his heart.

He returned full-body but half-alive. Living the same was not in his heart.

His soul had no heart.

God was not in his heart.

J.R. was tangled in the trenches, too, but he kept a candle with a small, steady light in his heart.

He shared the light with his troubled friend and they talked from the heart.

They shared their stories; they shared their fantastic tales of how so much comes from the heart.

Many heroes in their stories were mighty and strong but some were small with a sturdy heart.

J.R. and C.S. found a path to recover what was lost, and together they wrote timeless stories of the heart and for the heart.

J.D.

J.D. said, "There is nothing better than sand and sea."

His blond hair blowing in the wind as he scurried about the beach always looking at the sea.

His smile ever present; his energy endless, his eyes and mind were always on the sea.

Surfing and swimming when he could and talking about the sea.

One summer we asked about J.D. as we looked for him on the beach and waves of the sea.

They said he went down in the sea.

On a beautiful, sunny cloudless day he was taken by the sea.

He was lost forever in the sea.

Maybe it was meant to be, for he had a love affair with the sea.

Time versus Space

Time and space fight for our mind.

Time pushes space to the side, but space bends the mind.

Time tries to surrounds it and space laughs out of its mind.

Time is impatient and angry but space doesn't mind.

Time lashes out and space absorbs the mind.

Times screams at it but space buries it in the mind.

Time says it is eternal; space smiles and says, "Time in space is only in the mind."

Perfect Shape

The contours and shape are almost perfect.

How can a shape evolve with such precision and form so perfect?

It's difficult not to stare; the eyes are pulled that way to see what's perfect.

Her shy smile quickens the heart and makes it more sweetly perfect.

Dreams and heartbreaks are thinly separated by shapes that are perfect.

The shape lingers; the mind believes the heart; the memory is perfect.

Irish Island by the Irish Sea

The Irish island by the Irish Sea.

No land is more beautiful than Ireland by the Irish Sea.

The ancient land and the tales of ole ride forever on the Irish Sea.

Generations of good souls tried and true drift like ghosts eternally on the Irish Sea.

The Irish legends are not myths; they live in the currents and depths of the Irish Sea.

Late at night among the sounds of the past one can hear the siren sound of the Irish Sea.

Give in to her beauty; give in to her call; she wants to pull your soul into the Irish Sea.

Low

The stillness from the illness lays the heart low.

I stumble to my feet and feel the floor falling low.

I fall against the wall with its kindness to hold me up when I'm low.

I said to the wall, "Thank you," in my fevered state and feeling low.

The opaque sun streaks in to soothe my aches and slow my descent lower than low.

I walked for the first time in days around the room but my short journey didn't keep me from feeling low.

Illness is a thief carrying pain to render you low.

But low will not remain; just a few painless minutes restores my spirits to fight feeling low.

The stillness from the illness is the strength of life to counter the low.

Once Upon a Time

She was a little girl once upon a time.

A family that struggled and hid its suffering loved the little girl once upon a time.

Hunger and loneliness stole the love more than once upon a time.

A tender care and mother's love she knew once upon a time.

She dreams of those days once upon a time.

Under the bridge far from home she once believed in once upon a time.

Life turned away from her like people on the street who glance away not knowing that she, too, had hope once upon a time.

There were dreams, hopes, and an unlit candle once upon a time.

Once upon a time.

It Can Be Done

How many times will they say it can't be done?

Did Mendelson, Bach, Fulton, and Edison listen to the lament it can't be done?

List the reasons and rest on the reasonable for the source of all that can't be done?

Songs are written, poems are born, but children are told that it can't be done.

Everyone agrees with nodding heads that it can't be done.

They walk away self-assured and expecting nothing more because it can't be done.

She cried when they persisted that it can't be done.

They said, "Give it up and move on because it can't be done."

She wiped away the tears, listened to her heart, and said to the sky, "no one tells me it can't be done."

No fanfare or accolades are necessary because she got it done. No more time for "can't be done."

Echoes of Halls

The museum halls echo no matter how softy we walk.

Even if we whisper the walls watch us as we walk.

They are looks of disappointment that follow our walk.

Don't we understand the sacrifice and each life it took that allows us to walk?

The pictures, photographs, and statues wait for decades one day at a time to watch us walk.

But these are not only pictures, photographs, and statues. They are stories of people as we all walk.

They walk with us because the walk never ends. It is history's walk.

Quiet but Not Silent

The little boy plays with energy and joy but his world is silent.

His mother and father fear for his world that is silent.

They want him to enjoy childhood and have friends even though his world is silent.

But the little boy doesn't need the sounds of the world because to him the world is not silent.

What he fears is a world where love and caring and nurturing are silent.

Enjoy the little boy, be part of the love in his world; his world may be quiet but don't let it be silent.

Waif of Foreboding

The trench was spattered with pieces of life and smells of war.

Huddled together and bonded by fear, the young men tasted war.

They would be together for life, this one or another one, because of the war.

Their eyes may seem empty but their hearts are full of the pains of war.

Despair weaves throughout the trench, a waif of foreboding and an angel of war.

Her gentle persuasion feeds their hungry souls and over the wall, they go to die in war.

The poppy fields are now red like the memories of war.

Foreboding and loss are nectar to the angel of war.

Proud

A late-night walk led him near the statue, the opus of his life.

As he walked past, quietly proud of his creation, he saw an old man from his life.

In the dark, his elderly father stared up at the magnificent statue depicting life.

"Father, what are you doing? It's late and you have been sick much of your life."

"Yes, son. It's cold and dark, but your creation brought pride to my life."

"A man without pride has no place to go; now I can rest because I'm proud of your life."

Augustus Saint Gaudens and his father share a forever moment in life.

Mary Cassatt

Mary was devoted to her family and her art.

She saw life through the simple world of her life and art.

Painting became her life and possessed her soul of art.

While others thought flare was art, she felt the beauty of everyday life as art.

The touch of a saint, the eyes of an angel, the will of a god, and a master of the art.

She captured and nurtured the presence of every day in her art.

Purred and Pawed

Why do I still grieve for her?

The small bundle of white fur ran to me from the edge of the woods with no fear in her.

Precious to touch with cotton fur and wide blue eyes, the love of the world was in her.

Full of trust and longing to be touched, she came into my life in subtle ways unique to her.

She grew and played, purred and pawed, and longed to be loved for her.

She never came back while I was away – years later my heart still aches for her.

The pure love of her need for me stole my heart and it left an empty place for her.

Why Does It Have To End?

It has to come to an end, they all say it that way.

But why does it have to end in any way?

Why can't it keep on until other days are laid before us to show the way?

We don't pass it on to others because there is no way.

Everyone is different and times change our hearts, even if we want to keep it that way.

No, it doesn't always have to end; let it stay, let it continue this way.

She Waits by the Door

She waits by the door for spring to appear.

The cold winter and short days hold her too tight while she waits by the door for spring to appear.

The warmth of the fire doesn't shake the chill as she waits by the door for spring to appear.

Family and friends don't understand her heart as she waits by the door for spring to appear.

Enjoy the clear cold days; walk in the snow, but she waits by the door for spring to appear.

Don't miss the seasons of the year no matter, she waits by the door for spring to appear.

They don't understand her quiet heart; it's the warmth of hope and beginnings that keeps her waiting by the door for spring to appear.

Share His Smile

He smiles all the time in good times and even when it's a sad time.

Everyone shares his smile because it only seems right even when they don't value the time.

He brushed off ill-health to bad timing and the loss of a loved one to the stages of time.

His laughter fills the room and is a measure of time.

Each day fulfills him – a heart of kindness with no limits and unbound by time.

Time doesn't own him or move him or distract him but he values time.

The smile comes from a courtship with time.

Place of Peace

No finer place to be than a library at peace.

Each island of books is surrounded by trees of shelves and sounds of peace.

Find a corner to call your own and find a quiet moment of peace.

It's your world shared by writers and poets who watch their words surround you with peace.

The quiet gets quieter as the world of words pulls you into a world that knows peace.

Time stands still but the sunlight moves silently across the floor not wanting to disturb your peace.

When it's time to go, the feeling lingers; a new day coming will bring you back to your place of peace.

Doubt

It's a thief in the dark, a loud noise in the quiet, a cold blanket in the shadow.

Straight into your face or it clutches you from behind a shadow.

When it passes it's not for long; it just went around the corner to come back stronger in the shadow.

Shake it, spin it off but it stays around; like trying to run from your shadow.

It steals your heart and dampens your soul; it pulls you deeper into the shadow.

Even when it's weakened it will not go away; it lingers on the edge near the shadow.

Shine the light of courage into the dark of doubt and chase it back into the shadow.

Trees and Silence

They talk to each other in silence.

The trees learn what they hear and see in silence.

As we walk through the woods they feel our intentions in silence.

The trees know what we're thinking in silence.

If we think too painfully, the trees rustle their branches to distract our silence.

A creative thought spurs the trees to quieten the woods into total silence.

If you listen very carefully, you can hear the trees whisper in silence.

As you leave the woods, turn back to the trees and smile and wave; they smile in silence.

Mind Melts

The dream forms circles and colors and undulates and then melts.

It never takes shape; it moves closer to a shape but melts.

Like a sound far away that makes no sense, the colors dance and run together as it melts.

The colors have a taste; the colors have a smell; a blue color forms in the center and melts.

A slice of shape cuts through the colors and moves and spreads and then melts.

I finally reach for the shapes and colors to touch my mind, but it melts.

The Sandpiper

On the morning beach, I saw the sandpiper chase the water.

Even when I'm not there, the sandpiper runs to and from the water.

Rain, shine, or cold, the sandpiper rushes down to the water.

When man's tragedies engulf our lives and bury our hope, the sandpiper keeps running to the water.

Even if our heart is broken with loss and emptiness, the sandpiper waits for the water.

Our joys and sorrows are our own and the sandpiper doesn't seem to care by the water.

But knowing the sandpiper is there each day is the purpose – the sandpiper and the water.

Our grief and loss are taken by the sandpiper to the water.

Senator

He likes to pretend to care about children and others, but it's politics to him.

He wants to "think big" and "change systems" but nothing he's ever done has changed others or him.

Some people can't see the forest for the trees, but some can't see the trees for the forest that's him.

That simple-man veneer and good-ole-boy persona hide a cynical soul deep in him.

A self-described man of the people looks into his nightmares to face what is really him.

His days will end the same way as others like him – insignificant and irrelevant as we forget him.

The immortality he claimed is ashes on the rock blown away by a small breeze that abandoned him.

Idea

It appeared one day when I was minding my own business; was that an idea?

I don't think that way so it came as a surprise but it sounded like an idea.

I rolled it around in my mind and I put it back where it belonged but it bounced back as an idea.

It followed me around yapping at my mind, persistent and impertinent just like an idea.

I tried to brush it off and make it go away, but it claimed to be mine and it became an idea.

I gave in and put it to good use or so I thought, only to find out someone else had an idea.

That won't happen again, no more of that waste of time; I refuse to have another idea.

Oh, no, that gave me an idea.

Hallucinations Alone

He doesn't know what happened as he was carried off.

It was a light day full of sunshine with quiet time to drift off.

The hallucinations are not scary or new and he doesn't need time off.

He needs friends and colleagues, not isolation to cool off.

He copes by talking to his hallucinations; that's what sends the demons off.

But others thank he should be the one sent off.

Now he's alone with his hallucinations – a frightening thing that sets him off.

He can't get back to the ones that comfort his life because they saw him taken off.

With no one close by, the hallucinations are wrapping him tight and squeezing his life off.

This is therapy? Fuck off.

Her Smile

I guess it's a burden to smile.

That look of scorn has replaced the smile.

It used to carry me through tough times just knowing I could depend on the smile.

Now it's gone and I don't know what to do to bring back the smile.

My hope slips further away each day waiting for the smile.

The day I realized it wasn't coming back was the same day I forever lost my smile.

Time to Go

When did I start counting the days and years left to go?

The amount of remaining time was never on my mind because I was always on the go.

It was not my style to worry about what was left and how it would go.

One day I started counting backward instead of enjoying the years as I go.

Gradually the sun wasn't as bright; the rain felt colder; my step was slowed as I thought of how I would go.

I lost time waiting for it to end; in the end, it was time to go.

Priceless Time

We write when we're happy or when we're sad and no other time.

Most of our lives are lived in between that time.

And we don't capture those moments with verses about that time.

It's time spent living and discovering and living and breathing with time.

It's when we make and store memories, create energy and learn the value of time.

Take note of the plain and simple because that is priceless time.

Dolphin and the Sea

She rides on the crest of a wave in the dawn of sunlight.

She and the water are formed together like beams in the sunlight.

They sleep together in the moonlight and awake together in sunlight.

They play and hide, laugh and cry and they forever seek more sunlight.

One day she will go away but her spirit becomes the water shimmering in the sunlight.

The dolphin and the sea in the sunlight.

Purpose

Waiting has its own purpose.

We come into life waiting for someone or something to give us purpose.

Then we seek it with impatience and waiting hinders our purpose.

We kick and yell, scream and cry before we settle back into waiting for a purpose.

It was there the whole time we were waiting for the enlightenment of a purpose.

Waiting has a purpose.

Anticipation

A walk to the mailbox was exciting with anticipation.

The bills would be there, no doubt, but there was always the unknown anticipation.

A letter unexpected; a prize unannounced; a secret unknown added to the anticipation.

Holding our breath we opened the mailbox with tingles of anticipation.

Now we scoff at the mailbox - we are modern. Touch our phones and computers, but it's for the same anticipation.

Sunday Fear

Sunday evening fills with anxiety and fear.

When we're young it's the thought of school that raises the Sunday fear.

We anticipate and embrace growing older to displace the Sunday fear.

It doesn't fade away; its shadow stretches longer than the old Sunday fear.

As we grow older anxiety takes a new form of Sunday fear.

The melancholy of unfilled promises and dreams and the fear of time replaces the Sunday fear.

We're Old Cats

Old cat battered and scarred from life and living appeared one day.

Afraid to come close but still hungry and thirsty he stayed all day.

He devoured the food and looked tired most of the day.

Old cat settled in a sunny, piney place late that day.

Did he dream of old days, neglect and abuse from day to day?

Or did he dream of what could be – soft touches and food each day?

Do old cats and people dream of the past or what could be every day?

We're all like old cats at the end of the day.

The Last Time

Did you know it would be the last time?

When she danced with you and you both laughed did you know it was the last time?

When he sat on your knee and touched your face with little chubby fingers did you know it was the last time?

The walk in the woods when everything seemed quiet, sunny, soft, and clear did you know it was the last time?

Together you shared the wet perfectly shaped seashell on the warm beach; did you know it was the last time?

When you left her memory-filled house with pictures you gave her did you know it was the last time?

Do we ever know it will be the last time?

How would we act; what would we do; what would we say if we knew it was the last time?

Is the pain from not knowing it was the last time or is the pain knowing now that it was the last time?

Island of Green

When she was five years old the dream came to her as an island of green.

A mysterious dream of a mysterious place on a lush island of green.

Her parents smiled and said how sweet of her to dream of an island of green.

Through the years of dreams as she grew up dreaming about an island of green.

Walking and running and exploring mountains and streams on her island of green.

Even at the edge of death with the family nearby, she dreamed about the island of green.

The angel held her hand and led her to the island of green.

Politics and Children

The work was important and had to be done.

Everyone knew a wrong had to be righted and what needed to be done.

It was written and clarified and distributed so it could be done.

The outcome would protect children now and in the future so it had to be done.

"Wait a minute," someone said, this might cost money so should it be done?

The protection of children might affect the balance sheet so it can't be done.

But since it's for the children, let's be sure to take it up again next year to get it done.

A Child's Love

It's only one of a hundred we see every day.

It comes into our view but we don't see it in the rush of the day.

It's there for us to notice and cherish each day.

It doesn't ask for anything in return but it's there every day.

Sunday to Sunday, morning to night, a child's love is there waiting for us every day.

Nurse

She wakes up from a restless sleep after a series of tiring days.

She looks for the power of healing and comforting on good days.

But there are times when her efforts are not enough on those troubling days.

The pain is remorseless; the depression too deep; the hope slides between her fingers on those days.

The thought to quit creeps into her mind but her heart always prevails on those challenging days.

Looking into the face of someone seeking her comfort is all it takes to overcome the hard nights and relentless days.

The life of a nurse is the life of a saint who seeks only to comfort others in the day of days.

Time Matters

It slows down when you want it to speed up.

It speeds up when you want it to slow down before it speeds up.

It has a mind of its own without any care or concern whether you're down or up.

It will not change even though it changes all the time and never looks up.

It's stubborn and haughty and persistent no matter when we take it up.

It has no heart; it has no soul, but it controls our heart and soul whether we are down or up.

It makes us move faster and slows us down; it makes look at it all day and at night when we're up.

That's enough – your time is up.

A Fine Summer's Day

Irish whiskey, mulberry wine and a fine summer's day.

Under the trees with a slight warm breeze on a fine summer's day.

Nowhere to go, nothing to do, no one looking for me on this fine summer's day.

I can hear the quiet for the first time in weeks on this fine summer's day.

The noise of life is replaced with the quiet of life that we ignore each fine summer's day.

They are not infinite and we let so many slip away, each moment is precious on a fine summer's day.

The cold and dark will come soon enough and all we'll have left are memories of a fine summer's day.

So drink your Irish whiskey, watch the sun sparkle in the mulberry wine, and breathe in a fine summer's day.

From Far Away

It's almost here I know for sure.

It's around the corner almost in sight I'm sure.

It can't be late; it's too close to call and close enough to be sure.

There is no doubt; the world isn't that cruel of that I'm sure.

I can hear the train rounding the bend and churning toward just me I'm sure.

The train exists for me and no others I'm sure.

It contains a treasure far richer than anything manmade that's for sure.

She steps from the train like a shadow in a dream looking for me I'm sure.

Our eyes meet for the first time and we know it was right and sure.

The forgotten child from killing fields far away now feels safe I'm sure.

We smile and hold hands tight and sure.

Field of Sorrow

The photograph image of a day long ago filled me with longing and sorrow.

The man was young, his hopes high, but his eyes were filled with sorrow.

Why did his eyes forsake the moment with his family who were unaware of his sorrow?

Perhaps he knew what lay ahead both happiness and sorrow.

Happiness never quite measures the depths of sorrow.

The language of happiness cannot dull the severity of sorrow.

His eyes were mirrors of the future and his heart was filled with sorrow.

It was 1918 and in six months he would die in Flanders Field, the field of sorrow.

Alone

He lost his wife much too young and left him alone.

He raised his little girl as best he could all alone.

He devoted his life to her and made sure she was not alone.

She grew tall and confident and with so many friends she was never alone.

They said she was graceful, kind and gentle and avoided being alone.

He found joy in her success and her letters and visits kept him from feeling alone.

He grew old and she moved further away in her heart leaving him alone.

He understood and never complained as long as she was not alone.

She later found a poem he wrote her when she was a little girl; it was called "Alone."

The last line of the poem said, "With you in my heart, I can never feel alone."

She cried without end because she left him alone.

Dignity and Grace

She was ill most of her life and clumsy, too.

She broke her foot stumbling over a shoe but smiled, too.

She cut her lip on a cornflake cereal and dipped her hair in the milk, too.

She closed her hair in her school locker and fell down, too.

Her hair was always a mess and once she couldn't get the comb out of her tangled hair, too.

She was subjected to ridicule and mockery, too.

Slowly the lumpy body shaped up, the tangled hair grew rich, silky and smooth, and her pudgy face became porcelain smooth, too.

Though she changed in so many ways, she handled hurt and success in the same way – with dignity and grace, and she always smiled, too.

Distortion

The images are filled with people from the past.

Their faces are not clear and they move slowly as if held down by the past.

They open their mouths to speak but I can't hear anything but disjointed voices from the past.

The faces and the sounds don't match; the colors are faded and fading into an oblique image from the past.

Am I awake or asleep; in reality or in a dream; can I touch the present without being haunted by the past?

Is this the reality that slips away at times and retreats to the past?

How can I know if it's the reality of now or the ghosts of the past?

The Ache

I wanted and needed a rainy day to cover the ache.

I longed for the rainy day and the sound of rain that drowns out the ache.

A rumble of thunder overtakes the ache.

A streak of lightning splinters the ache.

And of all times the sun was bright and not a cloud in the sky to hide the ache.

So I took it with me into the bright sun and found the hottest place to melt the ache.

His Way

He always does it the hard way.

He knows no other way.

He won't try anything different because it's not his way.

Even with encouragement, he pushes it out of his way.

It's the highway or his way.

No compromise in his life to help him see a different way.

His family and friends slowly went away but he kept doing things his way.

Because the best way was always his way.

Now he's alone with his way.

His way.

Reality Room

Each door opens into a different hallway and then into a room.

Sometimes the door flies open without warning and I'm standing alone in a room.

At times I hear the door opening, creaking open slowly revealing a fear of what's in the room.

It comes in reality and sometimes in a distortion of colors and shapes in the corner of a room.

I catch the glimpse of a reflected image in the room.

What's in there; what's waiting for me? Is it new or an old hidden fear that now owns the room?

It's not going to let go, but it's only there because I know it's there in the room.

I can't let go of it and it won't let go of me. We are entangled in the grip of the room.

War Life

He wanted an ordinary life.

He faced all of the challenges of childhood life.

He survived the odd feelings and thoughts of adolescent life.

He labored over the decisions and temptations of a young man's life.

He wasn't looking for love but he found companionship to avoid a lonely life.

He settled into a job in his work life.

But the war wave broke over his life.

Totally unprepared he entered the Army that threw him into the war life.

Even when it ended he couldn't completely let go of the war life.

The dreams, the images chased happiness from his life.

He didn't share the visions or the crushing weight of the war life.

The weight grew heavier and the stillness overwhelmed his life.

It wasn't the noise of war that haunted his being; it was the stillness of his life.

He couldn't move forward to hear the beautiful noise of life.

He only felt the weight and stillness of a numb life.

He died alone; the quiet event was quickly forgotten by everyone's life.

Thinking

We seldom think about thinking.

It's only natural we say but that's not true about thinking.

It comes in many shapes and forms and it too often occurs without thinking.

Can we think without thinking?

The philosophers say we cannot exist without thinking.

The scientists say we cannot create without thinking.

Theology says we are not relevant without thinking.

What does it act like? Does it think before thinking?

Do we exist for the purpose of thinking?

My head hurts from so much thinking.

Change Cannot Feel the Warm

Long ago the island's beach was full, smooth, and warm.

Through storms and droughts, the nature of the island remained warm.

Even during sudden and turbulent times, the island was warm.

Wildlife sought and settled on the island to feel warm.

It embraced even those that had no feel or need for the warm.

The change is coming for the warm.

Change wants to consume the warm.

Change wants to be warm.

But change cannot feel warm.

The past, present, and future belong to the warm.

She Said

It's what they want, she said.

They want to feel free of me, she said.

I never intended to burden anyone, she said.

I would end it if I could, she said.

My freedom left, she said.

My dignity left, she said.

What is left? She said.

The human touch is all I need, she said.

One more time, she said.

Just one more time, she said.

Circles in My Mind

Circles in the mind.

Continuously rotating and spinning in my mind.

When I close my eyes the blackness is filled circles in my mind.

They will not stop circling bright in my mind.

With my eyes open I hear the circling in my mind.

It is constant now with eyes open are closed in my mind.

Shall I go mad or play with the circling madness in my mind?

I can ride the circles or be strangled by them in my mind.

Empty

When the emotional well drains to empty.

There is nowhere to go to keep the soul from being empty.

Then it's a dangerous time because soon the mind runs empty.

Decisions and reactions rising from a bed of dry rock are empty.

The skin shrinks; the muscles atrophy; the brain dies when the well is empty.

Some reservoirs are never full and consistently near empty.

I can't pretend anymore that it's full because it's empty.

I have always thought of poems as stepping stones in one's own sense of oneself. Every now and again, you write a poem that gives you self-respect and steadies your going a little bit farther out in the stream. At the same time, you have to conjure the next stepping stone because the stream, we hope, keeps flowing.

-Seamus Heaney

POEMS

"Dr. McGiboney reaches beyond the obvious and pulls us in with him as he journeys into a realm that defines why poetry is vital for mankind." - Frances Brouwnely, Irish Priest

"Beware of the seductive nature of the Timberline of the Mind. The poems seem simple and reassuring in their simplicity until you find yourself later thinking about the poems. Then it occurs to you that the poet has entered your mind." - Adarian L. LaCostauex, Poet

AUTHOR

Garry Wade McGiboney, Ph.D. has over 30 professional journal publications and is the author of several books on a wide range of topics. Dr. McGiboney has written guest columns for magazines and newspapers, and he has been interviewed by *CNN, NBC, CBS, ABC*, and many regional and local television and radio affiliates. Also, he was featured in a program for children on the *Nickelodeon Network* and on an *A&E* television special. Additionally, Dr. McGiboney appeared in a United States Department of Education video production for families that was broadcast on *PBS* and other networks. Dr. McGiboney has been quoted in *Time* Magazine, *USA Today*, *Los Angeles Times*, *Atlanta Journal and Constitution*, *Wall Street Journal*, and other publications, including the international press on many topics.

Dr. McGiboney is the recipient of several local, state, and national awards for his career-long efforts on behalf of children.

www.ingramcontent.com/pod-product-compliance
Lightning Source LLC
Chambersburg PA
CBHW060801050426
42449CB00008B/1486